Children of the Wolf

A Play

John Peacock

Samuel French — London
www.samuelfrench-london.co.uk

CHARACTERS

Helena Vincent, 42-year-old female, Robin and Linda's mother. She is well-bred, very beautiful, and impeccably groomed. Her clothes are expensive and tasteful

Robin, 21-year-old male, Linda's twin brother, Helena's son

Linda, 21-year-old female, Robin's twin sister, Helena's son

Michael Planter, Robin and Linda's father, Helena's ex-lover

Boy's Voice, offstage voice

1st Girl's Voice, offstage voice

2nd Girl's Voice, offstage voice

The play is set in 1971, and is performed without an interval

CHILDREN OF THE WOLF

First performed at the Dublin Theatre Festival in 1971. It opened at the Players Wills Theatre on the 15th March, with the following cast:

HelenaVincent	Yvonne Mitchell
Robin	Shane Briant
Linda	Sheelagh Cullen
Michael Planter	Joseph Conway
1st Boy's Voice	Brian Kelly
2nd Boy's Voice	Paul Keloe
Girl's Voice	Jacqeline Dunne
Director	Vincent Dowling
Designer	David Wilson

Bernard Delfont transferred the entire production to London, where it opened at the Apollo Theatre on the 31st of March 1971.

COPYRIGHT MUSIC

THE SET

A large room on the third floor of a Regency building. The building stands in its own grounds and is approached by a long, straight, broad avenue of cypress trees. One wall of the room is composed primarily of shuttered windows. There are two shutters to each window. Several panes are cracked or shattered. All of them are dirty.

The room is almost devoid of furniture. The only pieces that remain, hinting at a former glory are: a table, two chairs, and a small circular rug. All show signs of decay and neglect. There is also an old tea chest, spilling straw. The room is filthy. The paint is peeling.

The wall opposite the windows is completely bare, containing neither doors nor windows. In the remaining walls are two doors. One door leads to the main staircase of the building, has coat hooks on it, and a lock with a key. The other leads to a one-time ante chamber, which many years ago was used as a dressing-room to this master bedroom.

CHILDREN OF THE WOLF

*Early morning. The room is in absolute darkness. The shutters are
tightly closed*

*The first we are aware of anyone's presence is when Linda, standing by
the table, lights a cigarette with a lighter. The zip on her dress is undone.
On the table are a briefcase and a handbag. Near her is a travelling
bag. It is very large, of soft canvas, with an unzipped zip-top. There is a
garment protuding from it. Linda crosses to the staircase door, taking the
travelling bag with her. She opens the door and props it open with the
bag. The light from the doorway is only sufficient to light the immediate
doorway area. Once in the light, Linda attempts to fasten the zip on her
dress. She is somewhat shaken, but gains control as the dress is fastened.
She wipes her hands on the garment protruding from the travelling bag,
and replaces it. With a struggle she zips up the bag. She then returns
to the table and brings the handbag and briefcase into the dimly lit
area. During the following, she softly begins to hum "Happy Birthday"
absentmindedly to herself. From her handbag she takes a small, neatly
gift-wrapped parcel. She rips off the gaily coloured paper to reveal a
small, oblong, jewellery box. She reads a small card, accompanying
the present, laughs nervously, tears it up and drops the pieces into her
handbag. From the handbag she takes another card, similar to the first
and a pen. She writes something on the new card and places it on the box.
From the briefcase, she takes some more gift-wrap paper and proceeds
to re-wrap the jewel box and the card. She then finds some Sellotape,
some nail scissors and a ready-made ornate "ribbon-bow". She secures
the parcel with Sellotape and clamps the "bow" on the final product.
Eventually, she crams all the implements and the left-over pieces of
paper into her handbag. As she does this, the main door to the building,
three floors below, is slammed shut. Hastily, Linda closes the handbag
and the briefcase. She then puts the handbag and the briefcase on the
table , then the small parcel, thoughtfully, but quickly on the chair. Next,
she carefully removes the travelling bag from the door, thus allowing
the door to close quietly. We hear hollow footsteps climbing the stone
staircase. The stage is again in complete darkness but for the red glow
of Linda's cigarette, which brightens and dims, illuminating her face as*

she hastily gets all she can from it before dropping it to the floor and scraping it out with her foot

There is silence. The footsteps have paused beyond the door. Then, very slowly the door is opened to reveal Robin, wearing a coat, a small parcel in the pocket. He enters very gingerly, remaining in the dimly lit area

Robin (*whispered*) Linda...?
Linda (*relieved*) What?
Robin (*whispered*) Oh you *are* here.
Linda I've been here ages. I thought you were never coming.
Robin (*whispered*) I said I wouldn't be here till half-past eight.
Linda What you whispering for?
Robin (*whispered*) What you sitting in the dark for?
Linda The lights aren't working.
Robin (*quietly, anxiously*) They should be.
Linda Well — they aren't.
Robin (*slightly afraid*) Oh.

Pause. Robin is lit dimly by the open door. He is growing more nervous

Why don't you open the shutters then?
Linda I was waiting for you to get here. They're so old they'll probably fall apart.

Pause

Robin (*quietly, urgently*) Aren't you going to open them now?
Linda *You* open them.
Robin (*feebly*) I don't know where they are, do I?
Linda (*loudly*) All right then! I'll do them.
Robin (*loudly*) Don't talk so loud!
Linda (*whispered*) Well — stop whispering. You're making me nervous.
   (*She fumbles with the catch of one of the shutters*)
Robin Hurry up — it's dark.
Linda Don't be such a baby!

There is the sound of more fumbling from Linda

Robin What's the matter?
Linda You'll have to come and help me.
Robin I want to stand by the door.
Linda The catch is sticking.

Pause. Robin does not move an inch

I think — (*She starts to open the shutters, they creak as they open*) yes — there!

The shutters concertina back with a shower of broken glass, letting in the early morning light. Linda looks at the broken glass on the floor

Robin We've got to be able to see.

Robin gathers confidence now that there is light in the room. The palms of his hands are sticky. He rubs them on his trousers. Linda watches him, vaguely amused. Robin notices that he is being watched and is slightly embarrassed. They look at each other for a few seconds.

Happy birthday.
Linda Happy birthday.
Robin (*singing*) — to you. Happy birthday to you. Happy birthday, dear Linda ——
Linda Don't do that. Stop it.
Robin (*hurt, defensively*) It's customary. (*Then, quickly, singing*) — happy birthday to you!

Robin opens his arms, waiting for a kiss. Linda suddenly beams, laughs and comes towards him

Linda All right. You win! (*She pecks Robin's cheek*)
Robin The birthday spirit?
Linda The birthday spirit.
Robin And why not?
Linda Just thought it didn't seem right today somehow.
Robin You look pretty.
Linda You're sweating.
Robin I'm nervous.
Linda You always are. (*Indicating the shutters*) Come on. We'd better open these. There isn't much time.
Robin Not like my cold-blooded sister.

Linda has commenced opening another shutter. While she has her back to Robin, he notices the parcel on the chair. (From now on, until Robin eventually gets to opening the present, his eyes are forever on it. He can hardly bring himself not to touch it)

Linda What? (*She turns and catches him looking at the present. She smiles to herself and then turns to the next shutter*)
Robin A joke. I said — "I'm nervous — not like my cold-blooded sister". (*He laughs and cannot resist feeling the shape of the parcel*)
Linda Oh.

Robin replaces the parcel on the chair. Linda turns just in time to see him. Robin smiles at her

Robin A present.
Linda (*noncommittally*) Yes.

Robin waits to see if he is going to be allowed to open it, but Linda continues with the shutters. Robin shrugs, disappointed

Robin I'll help you.

Linda and Robin move along the windows fastening back the shutters, Linda slamming them home much more positively than Robin, who is being very gentle about the whole business

Linda (*considering the dirty windows*) Hmmm.

Robin sniggers

What's the matter?
Robin (*looking at the parcel*) Nothing.
Linda Better clear the broken glass. She'll be here soon. *Clean?*
Robin (*looking around*) What with?
Linda (*also looking around*) Oh — I don't know. Leave it then.
Robin Where shall I put my coat?
Linda Hang it up. (*She points to some hooks behind the staircase door, then she takes the parcel from the chair and transfers it to the table*)

Robin hangs up his coat. As he does so, he takes a small parcel from the pocket of the coat and slips it into his trouser pocket

Linda This place is rotten.
Robin Yes. (*Pause*) It must have been beautiful once.
Linda You mean when she came here?
Robin (*sitting down*) Yes.
Linda Don't be scared. Nothing can go wrong— (*she places her hands on Robin's temples*) — can it?

Robin (*suddenly animated*) No!

They both laugh. Linda stands to attention

Linda Did you post the letter?
Robin (*saluting*) Yes, ma'am!
Linda When?
Robin Yesterday afternoon!
Linda Which post?
Robin Three-fifteen.
Linda On the dot?
Robin Three minutes late in collection.
Linda Three-eighteen?
Robin Precisely.
Linda Which means she will have received it...?
Robin Twenty minutes ago.
Linda (*looking at her watch*) Twenty minutes ago.

Robin suddenly whips the present from his pocket and hands it to Linda

Robin (*proudly*) For you!
Linda (*feigning surprise*) What is it?
Robin Your present.
Linda But we said——
Robin "We wouldn't buy any this year." I know, but it *is* a special
  birthday. It's not much — more of a memento thing.
Linda Oh, thank you — I — I——
Robin Aren't you going to open it?
Linda Now?
Robin Well, yes. We haven't much time.
Linda All right. (*She neatly and slowly unwraps the present, finally
  revealing a jewellery box. She opens it to reveal a cheap, imitation
  crystal necklace. She deliberately over-enthuses*) Oh — (*She takes it
  from the box and holds it round her throat*) Oh, it's lovely.
Robin (*pleased*) Do you like it?
Linda It's beautiful. You shouldn't... Oh, Robin, come here. Come on.
  Come here...

Robin goes to Linda and receives a hug and a kiss in reward

Robin (*excitedly*) The card — have you seen what it says on the card?
Linda No. Where? (*She picks up the card from the wrapping paper*)
  Here.

Robin Read it — read it out loud.

Linda "To the prettiest, most beautiful sister in the world. (*Softly*) Ever my love. Rob." (*Pause*) Do you think I'm beautiful?

Robin (*shyly*) M — m — most.

Linda (*softly, thickly*) Thank you.

Robin and Linda look at one another for a few seconds

(*Breaking the atmosphere*) We'd better get ready.

Robin looks at the other present which is still lying on the table. Linda moves it to one side. She knows Robin is eyeing it

Robin Can — can I open it?

Linda (*taking some papers, notebooks and a pen out of the briefcase*) She'll be here in a minute.

Robin Can I?

Linda Can you what?

Robin Open it — the — *my* present. Can I open it now please?

Linda I — what do you mean, Robin? I said I didn't get you one. Not after we agreed.

Robin D — d — don't tease me, please let me. (*He picks up the present, rips off the crudely Sellotaped paper and greedily reads the card*)

Linda Oh that! No, please, Robin, that's not for you.

Robin (*reading*) "To the only girl in my life, to the beautiful Linda." (*He looks at the card, unbelieving*)

Linda pretends to be upset, feigning surprise. Robin is very hurt and jealous

It wasn't for me.

Linda No. I said it wasn't. (*Pause*) I'm sorry, but we *did*——

Robin (*upset*) Yes — we *did* agree. I just thought it would be nice.

Linda I shouldn't have brought it. It was wrong of me, but it was at the college, and I just wanted to get here quickly to you, so I put it in my bag. I forgot. Oh, Robin, I'm sorry. Really.

Robin (*quietly*) You'd better see what it is.

Linda I don't want to.

Robin See!

Linda opens the box. It contains a beautiful and expensive sapphire necklace

Linda (*feigning surprise*) Ah — a necklace! Looks like sapphires, Robin.

Linda watches the stony-faced Robin for his reaction

Robin (*flatly*) He must be very wealthy.
Linda Yes.
Robin He must like you a lot.
Linda I suppose so.
Robin What do you mean — you suppose so! Nobody gives anyone expensive presents like that unless he likes them a lot. He probably loves you.
Linda Don't be silly, Robin.
Robin Do you like him?
Linda I don't know. Come on. She'll be here in a minute. (*She begins to unpack the briefcase. She takes out a couple of pencils, two large rolled-up scrolls of paper, a shorthand notebook and some notes*)
Robin How long have you known him?
Linda About a year. Come on — help me.
Robin You've never mentioned him before.
Linda I didn't think it was necessary.
Robin I bet he's good-looking. You just didn't want to tell me. Is he... Has he a mother?
Linda And a father — and a brother — and a sister — and a pet dog. If I married him I'd have a ready-made family. Aren't I lucky?
Robin (*softly*) You wouldn't though, would you, Lin?
Linda Marry him? Course not.
Robin I bet you would.
Linda Silly.
Robin Does he know about you?
Linda Yes. If you're a deserted bastard, you might as well use it. It gets a lot of sympathy, you know.
Robin I think that's rotten.
Linda You could get a family easily. "Orphan Johnnies" are much more pitiful than "Orphan Annies".
Robin I don't want another family. *You're* my family. I want you.

Pause. Linda smiles to herself

Course, I suppose you've forgotten all those things you said about staying together and a home for us now that you've met him. (*Pause*) I don't think he really loves you.
Linda Stop worrying then.
Robin I'm not worrying. I don't like the sound of him, that's all. I bet they're not even sapphires in that necklace. I bet they're paste and glass.

Linda (*laughing*) Like yours?

Robin It's the thought that counts.

Linda Exactly.

Robin What's his thought, then? Trying to buy you! I'd send his necklace back to him. It's — it's an insult, and you — you're cheap throwing yourself at any man who gives you a sapphire necklace, even if it *is* real — and I don't think it is. What's more — why did you bring it today? You know what I'm like and today's such a *special* day. You're *spoiling* it! You're just ruining it all. *And* I bought you a present, which I took a lot of bother about. I think you could have got me something. You know what *I'm like*. You know I'd do anything not to upset you.

Linda *You* spoilt it! I didn't buy a present, because we don't *have* to buy each other presents, Robin. You and I are different. We've got something to do today. *You* had to spoil it.You have to turn the whole thing into a sloppy memory for next year. If you don't believe in us, then——

Robin (*interrupting*) *I do*. You *know* I do.

Pause

Linda Then prove it.

Robin (*slightly ashamed*) What?

Linda Show me that presents don't matter between us. (*She hands Robin the crystal necklace that he bought for her*) Smash it for me.

Pause

Robin It's a present.

Linda Put it on the floor.

Pause. Robin looks at Linda, seeing that she means it, hesitantly takes the necklace from her and puts it on the floor. He looks at Linda once more for a reprieve. There is none

Now smash it.

Robin It's a pre——

Linda Go on. Robin — I said "smash it"!

Robin hesitates for a second. Then he lifts his foot and brings his heel down on the necklace, grinding it into the floor

There, you see — presents don't matter. Now put this on for me.

Linda offers Robin the sapphire necklace. Robin holds back

I can't fasten it. It doesn't mean anything.

Robin slowly takes the necklace and fastens it around Linda's throat. Linda kisses him matter-of-factly, then breaks away from him

Where do you want the chairs? (*Indicating one of the chairs*) One here?

Robin nods. He picks up the other chair and places it down at the opposite side of the table.

Robin I'm sorry I doubted — us.
Linda Don't be silly. You should be thinking of today. See if she's coming.

Robin looks out of the window while Linda moves the chair to where she wants it and then continues sorting out the papers

Robin There's no sign of her.
Linda (*slightly nervously*) She's late.

Unseen by Linda, Robin picks up what remains of the cheap crystal necklace and puts it in his pocket

Robin She *will* come, won't she?
Linda Of course she'll come.
Robin She still looks quite beautiful, don't you think?
Linda She's a slut.
Robin (*almost hopefully*) She *might* not be a slut.
Linda She was then, she is now.
Robin (*apologetically*) I was only thinking. Sorry.

They wait in silence for a few seconds

Linda?
Linda (*bored*) Yes?
Robin You know you said you tell people that you haven't any parents.
Linda Mmmm.
Robin Well, do you ever tell them about me?
Linda No, of course not.

Robin (*disappointedly*) Oh. (*Pause*) I tell the boys in the shop about you.

There is another nervous pause. The two of them are now getting very nervous

You know — twenty-one years is a long time ago — I don't suppose...?
Linda We don't "suppose". She'll be here.
Robin Did you watch her yesterday?
Linda Yes.
Robin Did you notice the way she makes eyes at people?
Linda Mmmm.
Robin The postman.
Linda The breadman.
Robin The greengrocer.
Linda The paperboy — even the paperboy.
Robin He's only little.
Linda He's beddable. (*Pause*) Twenty-one years of eyeing, enjoying and not caring. She'll bring it all with her.
Robin It *will* be all right. She *will* come.
Linda Twenty-one years.

Robin puts his arms around Linda's neck from behind

Robin (*singing softly*) Lin's got the key of the door——
Linda But she *is* late...
Robin — never been twenty-one be——

Linda glances out of the window. She turns to Robin

Linda (*interrupting*) She's here.

Robin stops singing. They both stand, stunned, looking at each other, unable to believe the moment has arrived

Robin Is everything ready?

Linda nods her head, slowly, nervously. Robin wipes his hands on his trousers. Linda goes to him and holds his hands

Linda It *will* be all right. Just behave as we've planned.

The main door slams shut downstairs

Come on. (*She glances round the room once more*) Coat!

Robin takes his coat from behind the door. Some loose change rattles to the floor from one of the pockets. He stoops to pick it up, but misses one

Come on!

In a flurry, Robin dashes out on to the landing. Linda follows him, closing then door behind her

There is silence, but for the steady sound of feet mounting the stone staircase. The footsteps approach the door and come to a halt

Slowly the door handle turns and Helena Vincent enters the room. She is carrying a handbag and wearing a wrist-watch. She is excited and nervous, as though she is being both wicked and brave

The smile on her face disappears when she sees that the room is empty. Then she notices the papers on the table and her hopes revive a little. She crosses to the table and lightly flicks through the pages, but they are blank. She feels guilty as though she is about to be caught prying and crosses to the window.She takes a lighter and a cigarette case from her bag. Then she smiles to herself and replaces them without taking one. She looks at her watch and then crosses to the door, undecided as to whether she should stay or explore more of the building. Her hand is on the doorknob, when she sees a coin on the floor. She stoops down to pick it up, smiles warmly and goes to put it on the table. As she does so, she once again notices the papers. After a few seconds of indecision, she picks up one of the notebooks and glances through it. Her face shows puzzled interest. She turns a page and becomes even more absorbed. So absorbed in fact that she doesn't hear the door opening. She seems slightly disturbed by what she is reading

Linda quietly opens the door and enters. She has opened the door quietly but, having seen that Helena is reading, she closes it with a bang, and puts on an act as though she has been hurrying upstairs

Helena starts guiltily. She turns, expecting to see someone else, excited, but is faced with Linda, and is consequently very thrown by the encounter

I'm sorry. I didn't mean to make you jump.

Helena slips the notebook on to the table. Linda notices, but chooses to say nothing. Instead she tries to put Helena at her ease

My name's Linda — and you must be Helena Vincent.

Helena I — I — I wasn't expecting——

Linda You were expecting Michael. It's all right. I've got a message from him. He's been detained. He says he's sorry, but he'll be another half hour or so. I hope you haven't been waiting long.

Helena Oh — no — I've ——

Linda Good. I should have been here sooner, but you know what it's like when you're in a hurry — everything seems to go wrong.

Helena (*laughing nervously*) Yes, it does.

There is a long pause, during which Linda studies Helena, who manages to calm herself a little

Linda I don't know what we're standing up for. We might as well wait comfortably. Shall I take your coat?

Helena No, thank you. I'm a little cold.

Linda Well — sit down anyway. (*Indicating a chair*) This chair doesn't look too battered.

Helena sits down on the chair

Helena Thank you.

There is another pause. Linda offers Helena a cigarette. Helena shakes her head, and then changes her mind

Oh, perhaps I will. (*She takes a cigarette*) Thank you.

Linda lights the cigarette for her

There's really no need to wait with me. You must have lots of things to do.

Linda That's all right. I told Michael I'd keep you company till he got here. It's not a pleasant place to be alone in. (*She sits on the other chair*)

Helena Do you know Michael well?

Linda Mmmmm — yes, quite well — for Michael anyway. He doesn't really let anyone get "close" to him, does he?

Helena I don't think so, but I've been out of touch for a long time now.

Linda Really? You wouldn't think so. He speaks of you often.

Helena (*warily, excitedly*) Does he?

Linda Yes. How long is it since you last saw him?

Helena Oh before your time I should imagine.

Linda As long as that?

Helena We were practically children together. Tell me — what does he say about me?

Linda He says lots of things. He says you're very beautiful — very understanding, and — oh, yes — you're married to a financier, aren't you?

Helena I'm married to a man who happens to be a financier. Yes.

Linda I can't imagine that. Especially now I've met you. I mean, me — well — if a financier offered to marry me, I'd be very lucky, but you're worth much more. I'd have thought a husband of yours would do something exciting like sinking oil wells, or driving racing cars, or producing films.

Helena He finances those things. Isn't that exciting?

Linda If he's an embezzler.

Helena (*laughing*) You don't marry people for their "jobs".

Linda I just would have thought that your life was much more than stocks and shares.

Helena I think you marry someone because you love them.

Linda Michael used to own race horses.

Helena Yes. He had some magnificent stock when I knew him.

Linda Now, you see — *that's* exciting.

Helena If you're interested in race horses. He wouldn't do much for a stamp collector.

Linda And which are you? Ascot — or a penny black?

Helena Oh — I'm crazy about stocks and shares.

They look at each other. Linda breaks away, laughing

Linda I like you.

Helena Thank you — er — Linda?

Linda Yes. Linda.

Helena Are you married?

Linda No — but I want to be. (*Pause*) Mainly because of children. I want to have lots and lots. Have you any?

Helena No. None.

Linda I'm sorry.

Helena Why "sorry"?

Linda We were getting on so well together and now I feel that I've asked you an embarrassing question.

Helena You haven't. It's quite simple. I don't like children. I never have. (*She looks at her watch, rises and crosses to the window to change the subject, which has made her vaguely uncomfortable*) Oh, where is he?

Linda He should be here soon.

Helena (*looking out of the window, over the drive*) It's a beautiful driveway. So straight — and all those trees. In summer I used to love walking up that corridor of leaves and branches. The ground was all mottled where the sun shone through. I used to call it my yew tree walk.

Linda They're not yew trees, are they? (*She crosses to the window and looks out*) No, they're cypresses. They don't look anything like yew trees.

Helena All avenues should be made of yew trees, so I call them yew trees. I don't know what they are.

Linda They're cypresses.

Helena How boring.

Linda No. (*Laughing*) But it is a beautiful drive. (*Pause*) This is a strange place to meet someone you haven't seen for a long time.

Helena I suppose it is.

Linda Did you used to come here very often in the old days?

Helena (*laughing*) Yes.

Linda What's the matter?

Helena You ask me so many questions I feel as though I'm being interviewed for some sensational women's magazine.

Linda I'm sorry.

Helena I don't mind — really.

Linda It's just that Michael's mentioned you so often and I feel that I want to know so much more about you. *Did* you come here many times?

Helena Yes. The house was very beautiful in those days though. Very grand — luxurious — and warm.

Linda What was this room like?

Helena This room? Let me think — very different from today. The windows weren't broken. The walls were white — but there weren't any shutters. That's strange — no! I'm sure there were no shutters — unless they were hidden behind the curtains. It was a bedroom really, but the first time I saw it, it was being used as a cloakroom. Michael was giving a party — a fancy dress party, where everyone had to capture the spirit of the twenties. I opened that door and there were furs and feathers everywhere I looked. Literally everywhere. The place was smothered in ocelot — ermine — mink — boas — ostrich feathers, all catching the light of a huge chandelier, that hung over everything — and ladies with their "shimmies" and their beads and cigarette holders. (*She laughs excitedly*) You know, downstairs there was a band — just a small one, playing — let me think — *Limehouse Blues, Black Bottom* — all those kinds of songs — and the women were talking and moving in rhythm like a lot of birds — and flapping and fluttering and talking nonsense. I was astonished. Michael was standing behind me and he laughed. One of the ladies pretended to be shocked and chased him out of the room. (*Pause*) But it was a sight. I couldn't tell you what the furniture was — you couldn't see any. There were coat stands everywhere — not *just* coat stands, but large gilded ones that nobody used. They were all empty. My coat must have been the least expensive one there, but I *did* hang it up on a stand. The curtains were thick, heavy, deep, rich, honey-coloured. It was so — so luxurious and I wanted it all. (*She realizes that she has been carried away somewhat and smiles at Linda*) It was really wonderful.

Linda (*indicating the ante-room door*) What was through that door? It's all sealed up now.

Helena That? Oh — just a tiny room — a sort of ante-chamber.

Linda And...?

Helena (*uncomfortably*) That's all — just a small room.

Linda It must be sad now to see it all like this — all decayed and uncared for.

Helena No. Once you've known something as beautiful, it's always beautiful to you.

Linda You make it sound like a person. Anyway, I can't understand why he doesn't sell this place, if he's no intention of living in it.

Helena You might when you're older — and you think back on places that have meant a lot to you. (*She moves to the table. Suddenly, she recalls the notebook and the papers, which she has forgotten about*) But Michael *does* use this house.

Linda No. Not at all.

Helena (*looking at the notebook again; puzzled*) Whose papers are these?

Linda (*suddenly harsh*) I suppose after his wife died, there were just too many memories to live with.

Helena looks up

Did you know his wife well?

Helena No — not very, I...

Linda Wasn't she there on the night that you first saw this room?

Helena I don't remember.

Linda No, she was a very sick woman. She was probably in bed, listening to the senseless chatter and to the songs played by that small band. What were they? Er — *Limehouse Blues*? *Black Bottom*? They loved each other you know. She meant the world to him; he was very upset when she died. But, of course, you must know that.

Helena Yes, I...

Linda Michael knew she couldn't live long, but there was some sort of scandal just before it happened and I think that upset him more than anything — the fact that she found out.

There is a pause as the women look at each other

Helena (*very unnerved*) Do you know who these papers belong to?

Linda No, Helena, what are they?

Helena (*a little scared*) Just papers — but there's a notebook here.

Linda The papers are blank, aren't they?

Helena There's writing in the notebook.

Linda (*smiling*) Let me see.

Helena hands the notebook to Linda, who opens the book and reads a page at random

(*Reading*) "At eleven-thirty yesterday morning, she entered a greengrocer's shop just off Baker Street and enquired about 'kiwi fruit'."

There is a pause. Helena looks very tense and nervous. Linda studies her reaction, smiles at her, then continues reading

"This is the first time I have seen her, or known her, to shop personally. Normally everything is delivered or bought by the cook. Although impeccably dressed as usual, she seems nervous, on edge — a premonition perhaps?"

They look at each other in silence. Helena is frightened. Linda laughs

Some sort of diary. It's probably been here for years.

Helena (*softly*) It hasn't been here for years.

Linda (*matter of factly*) Now why should you think that?

Helena (*picking up her handbag from the chair*) You know it hasn't been here for years.

Linda Do I?

Helena I want to know what's happening. Where's Michael? Why isn't he here?

Linda He will be. Soon.

Helena I can't wait any longer.

Linda It's up to you, but if you care about him, you'll stay.

Helena I want to know who you are and who wrote that notebook.

Linda *Are* you going to wait for Michael?
Helena I...

Pause

Linda We'll answer your questions. What does a notebook matter?
Which is the most important to you — the notebook or meeting
Michael? I'm not here for your sake, or his, but if he means a lot to
you — and I think he does — then you must stay. But if you want to
go — the door's open.

*Helena considers for a few seconds, then she crosses to the window. She
stands silently looking over the drive*

You care and you will stay?

*Helena crosses to the table, puts down her handbag, and then returns to
the window. Linda sits at the table. She opens the notebook, picks up the
pen and commences to write, speaking aloud the words as she does so*

Tuesday, the fifth of September. This morning I find that she *does* care.
All is going as planned. She has decided to wait.

*Helena slowly turns to face Linda, who continues writing. Helena looks
on as though mesmerized*

For twenty-one years she has lived with doubt, camouflaged by lies.
She believes what she *wanted* to happen, not what *did* happen. Now
she has come to wait and remember the truth. The decision was hers.
If only — but then, she could hardly tell what the next few hours
would hold in store for her. If only she had decided *not* to wait — but
it is too late...

Helena looks frightened. Linda looks up at her

The door opens and Robin enters

*Helena moves a few steps towards him, but Robin turns the key in the
lock of the door and then puts the key in his pocket*

...the door is locked. She is alone with two people she doesn't know
— and there is no escape. (*She closes the notebook and puts it to one
side on the table*)

Robin crosses the room to stand beside Linda. Helena crosses to the door and tries to open it. She turns and looks at Robin and Linda

Helena Will you please unlock this door.
Robin W—we're waiting for Michael.
Helena I don't know who you are nor why you're here. I don't *want* to know. You can't keep me in this room against my wish so please open the door.

Robin and Linda do not reply. Linda takes out her cigarette packet, but finds it empty

Linda Cigarette, Robin.
Robin Er — yes — wait a minute.

There is a hold up while Robin takes a cigarette from the pocket of his coat, hanging behind the door, and gives one to Linda.

Helena Very well, we'll wait for Michael. He said in his letter he would be here by nine o'clock. He's not going to be very long.
Linda Sit down, Helena.

Helena does not move

I said "sit down".
Helena I will not sit down. Why have I been brought here?
Linda You weren't "brought" here. You came of your own free will — maybe because you love Michael.
Helena I love my husband.
Linda (*smiling scathingly*) Your financier? Your stocks and shares man? Do you really love him or is he, like your yew trees, a stand-in for what you want him to be? If you really feel so deeply for your financier, why did you come here today?
Helena I don't answer to you for any of my actions.
Linda You're going to answer every question we ask you.
Helena Why should I?
Linda Why should she, Robin?
Robin B — because the door's locked, because she's alone with us and because she's frightened.

Linda strokes Robin's hair

Linda That's right.

Helena But we *won't* be alone for long. You seem to be forgetting Michael.

Linda walks over to the briefcase and takes out a letter which she hands to Helena. Helena takes it from Linda

Linda Read it.

Helena reads it

It's a copy of the letter you received this morning. We wrote it and posted it to you, didn't we Robin?

Robin Yesterday afternoon. Three eighteen precisely.

Linda So you see, we *are* alone. You've no choice other than to answer our questions. Michael *might* be here later, but that depends on you, and has nothing to do with this... (S*he takes the letter from Helena and puts it back in the briefcase*)

Helena I think you'd better let me leave here immediately. This game has gone too far. What do you *want*? You're beginning to frighten me.

Linda "Frightening" you. We haven't begun to frighten you yet, Helena.

Helena Will you please unlock the door. My husband will——

Linda Your husband! Means nothing to you and you mean even less to him. That notebook doesn't start yesterday, it starts a long time ago. I'll tell you something. In half an hour's time, your little husband, your Peter, will sit at his large mahogany desk, move his pink *Financial Times* to one side and find, underneath, an envelope marked "personal". He'll look at the writing, pause with curiosity, and open it. Inside he'll find the letter he's been longing for since the day he married you, written on your cream parchment in your brown ink — the words he's wanted to see for twenty-one years.

Helena What? I...

Linda He'll know that he'll never see you again. He thinks you've gone away with Michael. It's signed "Helena". Robin found your small, cramped style was very easy to reproduce — much easier than Michael's. (*Pause*) So, Peter will heave a big sigh of relief and book a table for two with one of his secretaries. Which one, Robin?

Robin (*seriously*) I think the short one with brown hair, the one you think's ugly.

Linda Yes, the ugly ones are less trouble and *she* might be able to give him children. (*To Helena*) Oh, don't look concerned! Please!

There is a long pause. Helena moves the chair and sits down on it

Helena I came here to meet an old friend, nothing more, nothing less. Will you please tell me what you want to know.

Linda Everything about your relationship with Michael Planter.

Helena That was twenty-one years ago and has nothing whatever to do with you. It means nothing. Who are you? What is all this for?

Robin Shall I?

Linda Yes, Robin, read the first article of the notebook out loud to Helena, will you? Loud and clear.

Robin Yes.

Robin opens the notebook and starts to read, clearly if not too loudly, and slowly. This is the moment Linda has been waiting for. She relishes every word, watching Helena as the paragraph is read

"Medical Report on Helena Matthews. The patient was admitted to a South London Hospital on Friday September the fifth, nineteen-fifty, suffering the effects of a failed illegal abortion. An emergency operation on the patient resulted in the birth of twins, a boy and a girl, weighing four pounds two ounces and four pounds four ounces, respectively. Due to lack of oxygen during prolonged labour, the children were suffering from anoxia and declared 'at risk'."

Robin slowly closes the book. There is a long silence. Helena freezes, but appears to feel no emotion. She is fighting not to do so. She looks at neither Robin nor Linda, but stares directly in front of her. After a while she rises and walks slowly to the window. Linda and Robin follow her every move, but remain still. Helena looks out over the drive

Linda Can't you see any resemblance — or have you forgotten what Michael looks like?

Helena has her back to Robin and Linda. Silence

Helena (*quietly*) No — I can remember what he looks like.

Silence

Robin Linda and me. W—we're your children.

Slowly, Helena turns round to face them. There are tears in her eyes. She looks directly at Robin and Linda and speaks — gently, but firmly

Helena I have no children.

Linda You have no children. (*Pause, then bitterly; viciously*) You want to know why we've brought you here? We have spent the last twenty-one years of our lives being dismissed, being "conveniently" forgotten! Handed and passed from foster parent to home, from home to foster parent — to home — to the state! Each thinking how "good" and "kind" they were, manufacturing a "healthy environment" so obviously! And while we were growing up, hating every second of our charitable lives, what were *you* doing, eh? What were *you doing*? You were sitting back with your chocolate ginger and your kiwi fruit with your stinking fat financier, who you hated and who hated you, pretending that *we didn't* exist! Well from today we *do* exist! We're *here*! And whether you like it or not — you're going to *know* your children. (*Pause*) We want to talk to you. It's going to be a long talk, but even longer if you won't admit to yourself the obvious facts.

Helena (*quietly, but firmly*) As far as I'm concerned, I have no children.

Linda Today, just for once, you're going to have to forget things "as far as you're concerned", and see how the people around you have been affected — those you've chosen to forget. And we happen to be very deeply concerned that you're our mother.

Helena After twenty-one years I should have thought I'd given up that title.

Linda You're a very "convenient" person, aren't you? Get rid of the title, get rid of the lot! But you can't get rid of the responsibilities that go with it, nor the unhappiness you've caused by it.

Robin We *are* your children anyway.

Helena Any twenty-one-year-old in the world could be my son or daughter. If you say you are, then I suppose I must believe you. I didn't "dismiss" you because I wanted to. I did it because I had to. Just what did you expect from this complicated charade of yours? To frighten me and then watch me collapse when you told me who you were? Well, now I know who you are and I'm not frightened any more. I've never lain awake at night wondering what you looked like or what you were doing. Why should I? Twenty-one years ago I did what I had to do and the only thing left for me to do was to forget that it ever happened. (*More gently*) So you see, you don't move me at all. (*Pause*) I should have guessed when I saw that notebook. You must have been following me for days.

Linda Months.

Robin I followed you one day, and Linda followed you the next.

Helena I never noticed you.

Robin I thought you did once — in the greengrocer's shop.

Helena (*gently*) No — I didn't.

Robin Oh, I must be wrong.

Helena Could you please tell me now, Robin, where and when I can find Michael, then perhaps you'll let me leave here.

Linda Oh no, you're not leaving yet. I've told you. You'll be here for some time.

Helena Don't play games with me. I want to know where Michael is.

Linda He may be coming later. Now sit down.

Helena Why must you talk in riddles the whole time? (*Pause. Helena is beginning to weaken from her new found strength. Sighing, she sits down*)

Linda We haven't lied to you about our plans. Your husband will get a letter from us.

Helena Telling him he'll never see me again?

Linda Yes.

Helena What happens when I eventually *do* go back to him?

Linda You won't.

Helena How can you say that? You're surmising a lot.

Linda Not really. Deep down inside you know what we said about your marriage is true. You don't care for Peter and he doesn't care for you, does he?

Helena You don't *know* that. Anyway what business is it of yours?

Linda *All* our business. If Michael comes here and asks you to go away with him, we think you will.

Helena That means he *is* coming, otherwise you would never have dared to write that letter. It also means that Michael *does* want me to go away with him.

Linda Not necessarily.

Helena (*unnerved*) But if—if Michael doesn't come, there's no reason why I shouldn't go home to Peter.

Linda Just answer our questions. You'll find out soon enough. (*She takes a knife from her handbag and puts it on the table*)

Helena I've nothing to hide. I can tell you all you want to know. (*Looking at the knife*) I shan't become a martyr for my children.

Linda It can stay on the table. Maybe we won't use it.

Helena You say "we"?

Helena looks across at Robin, insinuating that he would never use it. Robin looks her back in the eyes, but gradually lowers his eyes from hers

Linda He's very shy. Robin's not like me. He really needed a mother. He's loved you all his life without ever having seen you. He's always given you the benefit of the doubt — lots of reasons and lots of excuses, haven't you?

Robin (*lamely*) No — I—I've always thought she was rotten.

Linda He's not a very good liar either. He's probably given you more good reasons for abandoning us than you've given yourself, but then he's not a Catholic, so he's got more scope. He couldn't wait to meet you today. "Don't you think she's still beautiful," he said.

Robin Shut up Linda.

Linda It's true.

Robin What you telling her that for?

Linda It's nothing to be ashamed of. Underneath all that wrong she's done, she might be the perfect mother.

Helena What do you mean "the wrong I've done"? Whatever I've done I've thought it has been right to do so.

Linda Right for you.

Helena Yes, of course "right for *me*" but right for other people too.

Linda I suppose it was right twenty-one and a half years ago, when, although Michael was married and you were engaged, you let him fuck you.

Helena I—I loved him.

Pause

Linda *Did* you? Well, I question that.

Helena Why else should I allow him to make love to me?

Linda Exactly, why *else*?

Helena Michael and I loved each other. If you think otherwise, then your notebooks and knowledge are wildly out of tune with what *did* happen. If you want to listen to my story then you want to listen to the truth, not some sordid little tale cooked up to suit your persecution complexes. Where *did* you get your information?

Linda That's between Robin and myself.

Helena Only Michael and I were involved. Any other source can't possibly be correct. I have a *right* to know and I *want* to know. Now!

Linda (*carelessly*) Oh we'll let you know. Later.

Robin Can we hear now w—what happened?

Helena I shall enjoy telling you, Robin. (*Pause. She rises*) Where do you want me to start?

Robin You don't mind telling us?

Helena Should I? Some of it is very beautiful.

Robin (*bewildered; looking across at Linda*) I thought——

Linda (*interrupting Robin*) Start at the beginning, Mother. Where did you first meet Michael?

Helena That's not the beginning. I heard of Michael long before I met him.

Linda (*thrown by Helena's willingness to relate the past*) Very well. Start there. How did you first *hear* of him?

Helena It was Peter who first mentioned Michael to me about three weeks after we became engaged. Peter used to travel to Sussex every weekend from London to see me. He was at university, you understand. Well, this particular Friday, he bumped into Michael on Victoria Station. Although they'd lived next door to each other when they were children, they hadn't met for three years, so they swapped addresses. Peter mentioned it to me when he got off the train and that's how I first heard of Michael. After that, Peter used to spend quite a lot of time with Michael and I got to hear more and more about him.

Linda Did you like what you heard?

Helena I didn't "like", I didn't "dislike". The only trouble was that Michael had a lot of money. He was very rich. He'd inherited a huge house and had everything that went with it. Peter suddenly decided he wanted to be like that. He spent a fortune going to the same tailor as Michael, joining the same clubs, but of course he couldn't keep it up for long. Then he'd talk about the big house *we'd* have with a swimming pool and a yew tree drive. That used to annoy me a little, but I didn't "dislike" what I heard about Michael. I just listened to the weekly reports while trying not to appear too bored.

Linda What bored you? Peter's talking?

Helena If I'd found Peter boring, I'd hardly have been engaged to him, would I?

Linda I don't know. That's why I'm asking you.

Helena Peter and I loved each other — at least we believed we were in love at the time.

Linda How many people have you believed you've been in love with? How many boyfriends did you have before Peter?

Helena I don't see what that's got to do with Michael and myself.

Robin (*quietly*) Please tell her.

Linda She knows what I'm getting at. Well, how many?

Helena (*a little nervously*) I had boyfriends at school, who I adolescently believed I was in love with — who I had a "crush" on. That's all.

Linda All platonic?

Pause

Helena I see. Yes. All platonic.

Linda So? And it was all platonic later, when you jumped into bed with Michael?

Helena We really loved each other.

Linda Wish you'd make your mind up. You've just said you "really loved" Peter.

Helena But I didn't, did I?

Linda You married him.

Helena Look, you said you wanted to hear about Michael and myself. I'm quite prepared to tell you, so why not let me and drop the dirty innuendoes.

Linda Why drop them just because you don't want to talk about them? We want to know if we were a product of what you call "a dirty innuendo". Were we?

Helena I loved Michael and he loved me.

Linda *Did* he?!

Helena Yes. He *did*.

Linda So Michael was the first?

Helena Yes.

Linda Why do you lie?

Helena I'm not lying. Why should I lie?

Linda Why should you? (*Pause*) You said you were bored by Michael's stories. Were you bored or were you frustrated by them because you'd never met him?

Helena It's difficult to get excited about someone you've never met. At least I find it so.

Linda But you'd seen a photograph of him.

Helena I — How do you know? I...

Linda Hadn't you?

Helena Yes.

Linda What was it like? Describe it to us.

Helena How can I remember? I'd forgotten all about it till you mentioned it. I think that it was of Peter and Michael.

Linda You *think*? It *was* Peter and Michael. Taken on their school sports day. They were sitting on the edge of the swimming pool. Arms on shoulders still wet from the pool. Puny sand-in-the face Peter, but Michael! Do you remember any better now?

Helena No, I don't, I can't——

Linda Those broad shoulders. That Mr Universe physique. Those iron hard thighs and the cock bulging in those brief, brief trunks. Wasted! Is that what you thought?

Pause

Helena (*softly*) You are filth.

Linda And you were engaged to Peter. How you waited for that first invitation. You'd been good for so long. Of course, you were a Catholic. But still — a crippled wife! Waste, waste...

Pause

Helena Be quiet.
Linda *Waste*! Am I lying or are you forgetting? But you'd seen the photograph and you knew he was married to a cripple?
Helena Yes.
Linda (*sing-song*) So, you weren't excited about him? You were still bored? And you weren't excited about meeting him?
Helena No.
Linda Where *did* you first meet him?
Helena Here, in this house on Peter's twenty-first birthday. Michael and Julia were giving a party as a birthday present. It wasn't exactly a fancy dress party but everyone was dressed as in the twenties. I told you about it earlier. It was the first time I saw this room.
Linda Was Julia at the party?
Helena No.
Linda Did anything special happen that night?

Helena shakes her head

Except that you ceased to be bored by Michael?
Helena Yes.
Linda But nothing happened? Nothing that made that night very special.
Helena I — no, nothing happened.
Linda Did you dance with Michael?
Helena Once, I think.
Linda Wasn't that special? Didn't it make you tingle all over? Even if you didn't think back to the photograph, he *was* handsome. Wasn't it that dance that started the great "*love*"?
Helena Yes, it *might* have been! But not the way you mean! There was nothing cheap about Michael and me.
Linda Love at first sight?
Helena Yes!
Linda *Love*? You'd only just met him! Was it love when he held you tight to him — or when *you* held *him* tight to you? Was it love when he rubbed his body against yours?
Helena We danced.

Linda Show us how you danced. Go on! Show us how you danced!
Show Robin and me how you danced! Dance! What was it — *Black
Bottom*?
(*Singing*)   Black Bottom,
                                      A new twister!
(*Speaking*) Oh, it was a hot night, wasn't it? Very, very hot. And he
was very close. Dance, you bitch! Dance!
(*Singing crudely, as a "bump and grind" number. On the second
"Charleston", she grinds her hips, swinging her stomach close to
Helena*)   I wonder does my baby do the Charleston
                                      Charleston!
(*Speaking*) Or were you feeling "Catholic"? (*She repeats the two lines,
crossing herself in rhythm, still suggestively*)
                                      I wonder does my baby do the Charleston,
                                      Charleston!
Helena (*turning away violently*) Don't *do that*!!
Linda (*laughing crudely*) Love?!

*There is a pause. A sudden silence. Helena turns to see what is happening.
Then Linda begins to sing, quite softly.*

(*Singing; softly*)   They call it Black Bottom,
                                      A new twister.
                                      It's sure got 'em
                                      And oh, sister.

Robin crosses towards Linda, as though through a crowd of people

Robin Helena? Do you want to dance?
Linda Thank you.
Robin I'm sorry I haven't had a word with you before, but, but all these
people...
Linda That's all right, Michael.

*Robin and Linda hold hands and pause as though waiting for the rhythm,
then they dance, ignoring Helena, but at the same time, goading her,
taunting her as they work the dance up to a frenzy, singing and laughing
at the same time*

(*Singing*)   Give it all that they've got.
                                      They say that when that river bottom
                                      Covered with ooze
                                      Start in to squirm.

                    Couples dance and that's the
                    Movement they use!
                    Just like a worm!

Robin⎫
Linda⎭ (*together*) Black Bottom
                    A new rhythm,
                    When you spot 'em,
                    You go with 'em,
                    And do that black, black bottom
                    All the day long!

                    They call it
                    Black Bottom
                    A new twister,
                    It's sure got 'em
                    And oh, sister,
                    They clap their hands and do
                    A raggedy trot.
                    Hot!

Linda   Old fellows with... (*Speaking*) What's the matter?

They continue dancing

Robin Where's Peter?
Linda (*looking over her shoulder*) He's drinking.
Robin Isn't it hot in here!
Linda Mmm...

                    They say that when that river bottom
                    Covered with ooze
                    Start in to squirm.
                    Couples dance and that's the
                    Movement they use!
                    Just like a worm!

Robin⎫
Linda⎭ (*together*) Black Bottom
                    A new rhythm.
                    When you spot 'em
                    You go with 'em,
                    And do that black, black bottom
                    All the day long!

They start to dance much faster

Robin (*speaking*) It'll be much cooler outside.
Linda (*singing*) And oh, sister,
                    They...
   (*Spoken*) What?
Robin (*slowing down*) Shall we go outside? It'll be much cooler.

They now dance considerably slower, and closer together. Linda tries to break away and speed up again

Linda What about Peter? I should be with him. It's his party.
Robin He's old enough to take care of himself.
Linda So am I.
Robin Don't dance so fast.
Linda Why?
Robin I want to talk to you.
Linda I can't hear you.
Robin Lets go outside then.
Linda (*breaking; smiling*) You win, but only for a few minutes.

Together, they move towards the bare wall

   Where we going?
Robin Only on to the verandah.

Robin opens an imaginary door for Linda to go through. Helena watches, stunned, motionless. Linda and Robin are now completely unaware of her

   See, I told you. It's much more pleasant out here, isn't it?
Linda (*restlessly*) Yes.
Robin You can come and stand beside me. I'm hardly likely to make a pass at my best friend's fiancée on his birthday, unless she wants me to.
Linda What do you want to talk to me about?
Robin You know — I'm clever, and you, you're beautiful. Let's talk about *us*, shall we? Do you find me attractive?
Linda (*turning away*) I think I'd better go and find Peter.
Robin (*swinging Linda around to him*) He's drunk. Do you find me attractive?
Linda I suppose you're handsome.
Robin I looked around the room tonight. You are the most beautiful woman here. I want you.

Helena suddenly rushes across the room. She tries to slap Robin across the face

Helena Stop it! *Stop it!*

Robin pushes Linda to one side and grabs hold of Helena's hand

Robin (*softly; to Helena*) I want to fuck you. Well...?

Helena tries to break free, but can't. Robin holds her towards him, speaking directly into her face

I told you, I'm clever. I've watched you. I can tell by the way you move, the way your eyes search constantly, the quick, jerky movements. How long is it?
Helena Please — let me go! Let me *go!*
Robin Come on, you need a man pretty badly — and I need you. Well? (*He presses himself against Helena, gyrating himself against her*) I need you...

Helena struggles, sobbing. Suddenly Robin loosens his grip. Still holding on to Helena with one hand, he mimes picking a flower with the other

All right, you can go back to your fiancé. You see this rose?

At the mention of the rose, Helena stops struggling. She stares at Robin

It's the first rose of summer. I want you to take it. I'll put it in your coat pocket before you leave tonight. When you want me, send me a petal and I'll arrange everything. That's all — just a petal.

Helena frees herself, slaps Robin fully across the face and backs away from him

Helena Lies. It wasn't like that. It's lies! (*She weeps softly*) He loved me.
Linda You couldn't get enough of it. You were and still are a nymph.
Robin But you sent the flower back, didn't you?
Linda Our mother has a raging, insatiable lust. (*Pause; then coldly, practically*) You're a nymph. (*She goes behind Robin and puts her arms around him. She strokes his thighs*) Look, Mother. (*Taunting; smiling, lightly repeating the phrase as though it were the refrain of a song*) You're a nymph. What does this do to a nymph, eh? (*She puts*

a hand between Robin's legs from behind, stroking him harder) See, Robin — those eyes.

> Those paternoster eyes
> Worshipping the thighs,
> The hard, firm thighs
> Of the paperboy.

Wriggle, Robin — wriggle!

Robin wriggles against Linda, who laughs and then breaks away after pushing Robin down on to the ground, where he blows kisses up to Helena

Because of her insatiable raving bloody lust, she begat two children. But because it was a Roman Catholic insatiable raving bloody lust — she tried to kill them, so that she could kid herself they didn't happen. But that didn't work. So she threw them away and pretended they never existed. She forgot them. Because of her aforementioned raving bloody lust she would have jumped into bed with Michael the first time she met him. But because that lust was Holy Roman, she had to convince herself that she loved him, that way the sin wasn't *so* bad. But she became heavy with child and he made her sin again. He made her abort and all for nothing! Because he didn't love her. You sinned. You fornicated, Mother. (*Lightly*) Why didn't you kill yourself? I would. Why *don't* you kill yourself? What gets you going, Nymphy?

Linda moves to Helena and begins to play with her hair from behind. Helena remains motionless

This? Does it matter if it's a man or doesn't it matter, as long as it's good firm flesh?

Linda puts her hands on Helena's breasts and caresses them as she moves around to face her. Suddenly, it is almost as though Linda herself is enjoying the sensation. Then, all at once, she pushes against Helena, with all her force. Helena winces with pain and sinks to the floor, holding her breasts and sobbing

Helena Don't. Don't hurt me — please?
Linda Are you a nymph? (*Pause*) Helena, I want to hear you say you are. I want you to admit it. Confess it to *me*. Are you — a — nymph?

Helena Please?

There is a silence. Linda looks at Helena, then very slowly, she walks across to the table. Equally slowly, Linda picks up the knife. She crosses to Helena and stands behind her

Linda Robin and I were born suffering from anoxia. Do you know what that means, Mother? (*She gently draws the blade of the knife through Helena's hair*) It means that because of your pathetic attempt to get rid of us far too late, you went into prolonged labour while *we* lacked oxygen. (*Pause*) That's what they call "anoxia". Because of that we were declared — what was it Robin?
Robin (*stepping forward*) At risk.
Linda At risk. That means we can't be adopted. Well, you can't expect to be I suppose. Chances are lack of oxygen during labour leads to permanent brain damage. (*She crosses to Robin*) Do you think we were affected, Robin?
Robin No.

Linda is delighted by his seriousness. She holds his head against hers, still looking at Helena for her reaction

Linda Isn't he cute? He's like a little baby. He's afraid of the dark even. He'll do anything I ask him, won't you baby? Together?
Robin Together.
Linda Anything I ask him. (*She suddenly turns to Helena and walks slowly towards her. She is still holding the knife. Pause; to Helena*) Now are you a nymph?

Helena does not reply

(*Calling to Robin; not looking at him*) Come here, Robin.

Robin moves to stand beside Linda. Linda raises the knife, then she lowers it swiftly towards Helena and tears open the front of her dress. Then she stands back.

Play with her, Robin.

Helena's eyes move to look at Robin. There is a long silence. Linda's eyes never leave Helena

Robin.

Robin Yes — I...
Linda You and me are together. You know what I want you to do.

Robin nods

   Then play with her.

Robin moves slowly towards Helena. Linda backs away further, smiling.
Helena looks at Linda. Robin kneels down beside Helena. He pulls away
the torn section of the dress. Helena turns to look at Robin. Their eyes
meet

Helena You're my son.

Pause

Linda Robin.

Robin looks pleadingly at Helena. There is a long stillness. Then, Robin
puts his hand inside the dress. Helena groans. She pushes Robin's hand
away, gently

Helena (*softly*) I am what you say I am.
Linda Say "I am a fornicating nymph. I have sinned against my church
   — against God".
Helena (*calmly*) I am a fornicating nymph. I have sinned against my
   church, against God.

Pause. Robin steps back from Helena, turning away from her. Helena
pulls her dress together and looks at Linda, who laughs viciously

   (*Continuing; quietly*) Yes, I am what you say I am, but you made my
   son do that to his mother. I am glad I'm not you.
Linda Get up!

Helena struggles weakly to her feet, trying to regain some composure

   Did Peter know what he was engaged to? No — for him you were
   good. For him you were a twelve-year-old convent school girl.
Helena (*flatly*) I've told you what I am. Isn't that enough? I didn't want
   to be. I tried to be faithful for Peter. I really tried.
Linda It must have been an effort after all those men. How many was
   it? Ten, twenty, fifty? How many before you stopped your prancings

and met Peter? For him you tried, you really tried. You tried and you tried, but you met Michael and you failed. You lusted for Michael, didn't you? You didn't love him. From the first moment you saw his photograph, you *lusted* for Michael! (S*he crosses to Helena; smiling*) And you fell.

Helena Yes, all right — yes! But only because he loved me. Whatever you may think, he loved me.

Linda If you say that often enough you might even believe it.

Helena crosses to the window, her back to Linda and Robin

Helena (*softly*) No. Those before Peter, they weren't for "love", but, whatever you may think, Michael was. I think I'm more qualified to know the difference between lust and love than you. (*Pause. Suddenly very cool and controlled; speaking with authority*) Give me a cigarette.

Linda Robin.

Robin lights a cigarette and gives it to Helena. Helena draws on it and then turns to face them

Helena You think I *enjoyed* those days before Peter? I would beg anyone to spend a night, an hour with me. When I was eighteen — younger than you — I used to wake up night after night with someone I'd never known ten hours before. They treated me like a whore. My payment was satisfaction, which I never got. I was sick — I used to *be* sick. Sick of what I was, sick of what I was doing — sick of it all! They knew what I wanted and they took what pleasure they could from it. Then I met Peter. *He* loved me. From the beginning he never touched me and swore he wouldn't till we were married. There was a reason for that. Michael was the only person who loved me and enjoyed me for what I was.

Linda Or did he want you like those others for what he could get out of you? He loved Julia.

Helena He was sorry for Julia. He loved me.

Linda Then why didn't he leave Julia, when you were pregnant, and go away with you?

Helena He would have done if I'd asked him, but how could I? Julia was a cripple. She depended on him for everything.

Linda But you *did* ask him to leave her and go away with you, didn't you?

Helena No, I wouldn't — I didn't.

Linda You *did*, Helena.

Helena No! I couldn't——
Linda How did you put it?
Helena I *didn't*!
Linda (*screaming*) *Michael*! MICHAEL!

Robin slaps Linda across the face

Robin For God's sake shut up! She'll hear you.
Linda She'll hear me? So? She'll hear me! Let her! It's not *her* who's carrying your baby, it's me! (*She puts her arms around Robin and pleads with him, urgently, softly*) Please, please Michael, I don't know what to do. You've got to look after me, you've *got* to. Come away with me. Please...?
Robin Julia needs me.
Linda Don't you think I do?
Robin Julia is my wife, Helena. I'm married to her.
Linda Was it ever consummated?
Robin Don't be a bitch!
Linda She's a cripple. Cripple. *Cripple*! CRIPPLE!
Robin Shut up!

Linda cries

Robin (*gently*) I can't leave her.
Linda I love you.
Robin I know you do. But you also know about Julia; you always have.
Linda But I'm pregnant.
Robin Then we'll have to arrange an abortion.

Pause. Linda looks up at Robin, shaking her head, stunned

Helena No, no — no — not that.
Linda (*mumbling*) ...no — no — no — not that. If you don't come away with me I — I'll tell Julia all about us.
Robin Even you wouldn't do that. You wouldn't sink that low.
Linda I'm not having an abortion, Michael —I'm *not*!

Linda whirls round. Robin moves away leaving Linda standing alone. Helena is sobbing quietly. Linda moves across to her as though Helena were Julia

Linda Excuse me — Julia?

Helena No — no, all right. Yes! I did — I did!

Linda Julia, I want to talk to you. It's very difficult for me to tell you like this——

Helena Stop it!

Linda —but however much it hurts you, you've got to know. I can't help it. I love Michael and he loves me.

Helena I was wrong. I shouldn't. I shouldn't, but I paid. I paid for it. Please, stop...

Linda I'm pregnant. I'm carrying Michael's baby and I want you to let him come away with me, or let me live in this house. He doesn't love you. He feels sorry for you, because of what you are. He won't tell you himself. But he loves me really, and *we* have a baby.

Helena is in a state of near hysteria, staring at Linda, tears pouring down her cheeks

Robin (*suddenly darting forward*) Listening as you played music. Hearing the laughter, but not the joke — and how she must have wept when the music finished.

Helena She didn't know. You're just hurting. You're lying.

Linda And her bedroom that looked over the drive — the avenue of *her* cypress trees. She listened, watched, and knew — but she kept herself alive by pretending that those things never happened. You proved to her that day, that they *did* happen and three months later, Julia was dead.

Helena No — mmmm — no — it wasn't like that. It wasn't because of me.

Linda (*coldly*) You killed her.

Helena She was ill. She was — she...

Linda You killed her and you also lost Michael. Even if he would have gone away with you before, he couldn't then. Yes, because you told Julia, he had the excuse he needed. He could tell you he loathed you with justification. He could get rid of you once and for all. It had gone on too long anyway.

Helena Yes, all right, I shouldn't have told her; but he still loved me. He did. He did.

Linda Does a man who loves a woman, really, properly, tell her to have an abortion — tell her to kill what they created together? Would he ask her to rip her inside out? Well, would he?

Helena He loved me. He loved me.

Linda He *had* to as far as you were concerned. The cost was too great. If you don't believe that, your life isn't worth living, is it? Julia, us, Peter, your own Catholic conscience — *all* for nothing!

Helena (*firmly*) I know he loves me.
Linda If he does love you, he'll be here within the next half hour.

Helena looks up at Linda

If he doesn't love you, then he won't be here — which means it was all
for nothing. And if all this suffering *you* have caused was for nothing
we're going to kill you.

*A long silence. Helena looks first at Robin, then at Linda. Linda smiles
back at her and then slowly begins to walk around Helena, singing
softly*

(*Singing*)   Kill — kill — kill you.
                     Kill — kill — kill you.

                     Black Bottom,
                     A new twister.
                     You sure got 'em
                     And oh, sister,
                     You clap your hands and...

                     Kill — kill — kill...

(*Stopping and turning to face Helena; speaking*) What's the matter
"Mother", don't you believe us? You killed Julia and you tried to
kill us. Why shouldn't we do the same to you? Course, if he loves
you, then you won't die. (*Pause*) I've waited for this; you know that?
Daydreamed it all, step by step, minute by minute. I've lived through
the last sixty seconds of your life so many times, waiting for him and
wondering what would happen if he didn't come. Would you be stoic,
Mother, or would you grovel and plead? Would we have to stop you
screaming? Twenty-five minutes to go. (*Pause*) I hope he doesn't
come — I want to watch you die.
Helena Kill me?
Linda (*studying Helena*) Hmmmm.
Helena My — Michael's and my — children.
Linda Yes. Your children. You should have made sure that we never
lived. "Ironical", that's the word, isn't it? "Ironical". You should have
stamped out the dirt in your life while you were able, then you could
forget your bungling little mistakes, but you even had to bungle your
abortion. (*Pause*) Robin and I don't make mistakes. We don't "bungle"
things. If Michael doesn't arrive by ten o'clock, we shall kill you.

Helena I believe you *would*.

Linda We *shall* — if — *if* — IF...

Helena (*simply*) He'll be here.

Linda You're not sure though, are you? Not at all.

Helena I'm sure — providing you're telling the truth and he does know I'm here.

Linda Oh, he knows.

Helena How does he know? Did you write a letter to him, Robin?

Robin No. It was Linda. She ——

Linda I wrote to him and I know he received it yesterday morning because he told me. Michael and I have very few secrets from each other. If you see what I mean.

Helena So your fictions don't end with my past.

Linda Why should it be a fiction? Why shouldn't he know me as well as he knows anybody? *You* liked me at first. We "got on"! Michael and I get on just that little bit more. He actually *likes* me as he likes *all* young women. He doesn't know I'm his daughter, just that I'm a young, attractive woman with no complications, single, atheistic and relatively free. Everything that he looked for in you. He wants to make love to me, but he is my father. (*She laughs, throwing even more innuendo on the statement*) Aren't you jealous at the thought of him making love to other women? He does you know, frequently. Do you feel betrayed?

Helena No. That's not betrayal. Michael wouldn't betray me.

Linda What about the results of your torrid little affair then, eh? Two children who want to kill you, a dead wife, and a promiscuous lover of late. (*Pause*) You wanted to know where I learnt so much about you and your past.

Helena Well?

Linda From the only other possible true source — Michael.

A stunned pause

Helena I don't believe you.

Linda Then how else do I know? Every other day I saw him, didn't I, Robin? Every other day.

Helena I don't believe you!

Linda I know him better than I've claimed so far. (*Quietly; sincerely*) He's told me that he loves me. Apart from you, I am the only woman he has ever loved.

Helena I——

Linda (*breaking the mood*) Doubt — doubt — doubt! (*Then, seriously again*) I mean it.

Robin Linda!

Linda What's the matter, Baby Bunting, are *you* jealous as well?

Robin You never said that——

Linda That Michael was "fond" of me?

Robin Yes.

Linda I didn't say that I was fond of him either, did I?

Robin You're not. You, you weren't!

Linda I wasn't. That's right. (*She laughs and crosses to Robin and strokes his hair*) It was a one-sided little affair. (*To Helena, softly, simply*) I couldn't tell, you see. I wasn't sure whether he loved me or whether he just wanted to get me into bed with him. I didn't particularly "feel" anything towards him except it was nice, or it would have been nice, to have somebody crazy about me — someone who really *did* care for me.

Robin I do, Linda. I care for you. (*He goes to Linda and puts his arms around her neck*)

Linda Hmmm! You *need* me. It doesn't matter. It's over. I wonder if he'd have liked me so much if he'd known that I was his daughter? The only way I could have found out was to tell him and that would have spoilt everything.

Helena You say it's over.

Linda The next time we meet I shall tell him, which will be very soon. I told him that you were coming here this morning and that it was his one chance to see you. But I made it clear that if he *did* come, then he would never see me again. (*Pause*) So, you see. It's either you or me. The only two women he has ever loved, if we can believe him. He has a choice between the past and what he thinks could be the future. Which will he choose?

Helena He'll come here to see me.

Linda How do you know?

Helena Because of a token.

Linda What kind of a token?

Helena A promise we made.

Linda For what?

Helena For the future.

Linda Tell us about it. Tell us about your pathetic keepsakes! Your "token"!

Helena Why should I? I don't have to "prove" anything. I don't believe your story.

Linda What was it a token of?

Helena Of the times we spent — of one special time.

Linda What time? Tell us! Or are you afraid we'll prove it's something else that you *wanted* to happen, and not what *did* happen.

Helena No, I'm not afraid of that. (*Pause*) Very well. I'll tell you. (*Pause*) When we were alone together, Michael and I, we created a world of our own. A world of yew tree walks — a world without Peter or Julia — which only we shared. It was ours. We lived in the future, that one time when we could perhaps be together as man and wife. Then, Julia went away into the country for a fortnight. Michael stayed in London, and for those fourteen days the future became the present and we *did* live together. It was during that time, Robin, I conceived. On our last day we went shopping together. Michael said that I was to choose a present for myself and then give the present to him. Similarly, he was to choose a present for himself and give it to me. Then on the day that we became free, free to live as we had lived during that past fortnight, we would meet and exchange our gifts. We swore solemnly that we would keep them through the years, whatever happened. We took them home and carefully wrapped them. Michael had chosen for himself a pair of diamond-studded cuff-links. I've brought them with me today. Still wrapped as he wrapped them all those years ago.

Robin You promised you would keep them safe until you...

Helena Yes.

Robin Has he still got the present that you chose for yourself?

Helena Yes. As he loves me.

Robin What was it?

Helena It was a beautiful sapphire necklace.

There is a pause. Robin looks across at Linda, puzzled

Linda Like this?

Linda takes the necklace from the front of her dress so that Helena can see it. Helena gasps and begins to crumble

Michael gave me it for my birthday. As Robin said, whoever bought it must think an awful lot of me to buy such an expensive present. (*Pause*) Is it very similar to yours? (*Pause*) It looks as though it's real sapphires, but it's probably paste and glass — don't you think? Have a closer look. You can hold it if you like. (*She begins to unfasten the necklace*) It would look lovely around your throat. You've such a pretty neck! I'd like you to wear it for a while. That would be fun, wouldn't it Robin? Wouldn't it be fun if we let our mother wear our most treasured possession, eh?

Robin You told me, you—!

Linda Shut up, Robin! Wouldn't it be fun? Unfasten it for me and put it on Helena.

Helena looks directly ahead as Linda bends towards her

You sure it doesn't look like the one you chose?

Robin removes the necklace from Linda and approaches Helena

Beautiful, isn't it?

Helena How did you get it?

Linda Told you. Birthday present. He loves me! He loves me! Isn't it beautiful? Put it on for her, Robin. (*Laughing*) You may keep it. A present from you to Michael to me to you!

Robin (*fastening the necklace on Helena*) Is it?

Linda What?

Robin Is it a present from Michael to you?

Linda (*irritated*) Of course it is.

Robin You said — you *know* what you said.

Linda I said it was a present from someone at college.

Robin Yes.

Linda Well?

Robin Well now you say that it's from Michael.

Linda I was lying.

Pause

Robin You can't — you can't! Together! We're together!

Linda I did, though, didn't I?

Robin Why?

Linda Because I know what you're like. Michael gave it to me yesterday. I saw him yesterday afternoon. I didn't go to college as you thought. I see Michael far more than I say I do. I lie because I can't bear these scenes with you. That's all. Now, shut up.

Pause

Robin I tell you everything.

Linda How do I know?

Robin I do! You should have told me! You should! (*Pause*) I don't lie to you.

Linda You don't have to. I'm not jealous of you, am I?

Pause

Robin Don't — don't you c — care?

Linda (*smiling*) Not when today's over, no.

Robin crosses to the door

> You can't go now, Robin. (*She moves behind Helena and puts her hands on Helena's shoulders*) Since as long as we can remember you've planned this. This one day — you can't leave now. After, maybe, but not during.

Robin It wasn't because — because of looking forward to today that kept me with you, Linda. It was the looking forward to *after* today.

Robin takes his coat from behind the door. He takes the key from the pocket and fits it into the lock. Linda stops smiling when she realizes that Robin might actually be leaving

Linda Robin?

Robin looks at her, then he unlocks the door and opens it

> You don't have to, Robin. You don't *have* to go. I care. Of course I care. You shouldn't have to ask me. (*She crosses to Robin and puts her hands on his face*) Please don't go — please stay. (*She tenderly kisses him*) You believe me, don't you?

Robin (*crying*) No. (*He closes the door*) No, I don't believe you——

The main door three floors below is slammed shut

Linda Robin!

Robin moves away from the door not knowing what to do. Linda pushes him to one side

Helena (*softly*) Michael — I knew — Michael...

Linda (*to Robin*) Keep her quiet, Robin.

Robin But I——

Linda Keep her quiet! (*She re-locks the door and pockets the key*) Stay very still and don't make a sound (*She takes the knife from the table, crosses to Helena and holds the knife against her wrists*)

Robin Linda...

Linda Sssssh!

We hear footsteps scuffling on the stairs. We hear someone banging on the door of the room underneath

Robin What's he doing?
Linda Be quiet!

There is a pause, then we hear footsteps approaching the door

Helena Mich——!

Robin clamps his hand over Helena's mouth. There is a pause outside. The door knob is rattled backwards and forwards

Girl (*off*) Jimmy! Jimmy! Jimmy!

Robin looks at Linda puzzled. Helena reacts on realizing that it isn't Michael. We hear the sound of someone running upstairs to join the first girl

Boy (*off*) What's the matter?
Girl (*off*) 'S locked as well.

The door is rattled again. The three in the room are very tense. Through the next passage we hear the 2nd Girl coming up the stairs and approaching the door

Girl (*off*) Told you. 'S locked.
Boy (*off*) Wasn't yesterday.
Girl (*off*) 'Tis now. (*Calling*) Sally!
2nd Girl (*off*) What? Where are you?
Girl (*off*) Up here. 'S locked.
2nd Girl (*off*) You sure?

The door is rattled again. Helena winces

Girl (*off*) See!
Boy (*off*) Might have bin a copper.
2nd Girl (*off*) I'm scared.
Boy (*off*) He might still be here — hiding. He might jump up and have you! *Look out!*

There is the sound of stampeding feet as the Boy and the Girl run upstairs. The 2nd Girl goes, but screams excitedly

2nd Girl (*off*) Come down! *Stop it!*

Linda gives the knife to Robin

Linda I'll turn them out. Give me the key.
Robin You've got it.

Linda fishes the key out of her pocket. From upstairs we hear the Boy laughing horrifically

Boy (*off*) Behind you! *Aaaaagh!* He's coming to getcha, Sally!

We hear the 2nd Girl crying. Linda very slowly unlocks the door. She turns to Helena, indicating the knife. We hear the 2nd Girl scamper upstairs to join her friends

Linda We don't want to harm the children — you understand?

Linda goes on to the landing. She closes the door and locks it behind her. Robin indicates to Helena that she should sit on a chair. He removes his hand from her mouth and almost gently, leads her to the chair

Robin There.

Helena sits. Robin then stands beside her, with the knife apparently "ready", should she scream. There is a long silence between them, during which Robin moves to face her. All we can hear from the rest of the building are vague noises. Helena runs her hand over her face in a calming motion. Her hand then moves down to her throat, where she feels the necklace. She very slowly unfastens it and holds it across her lap. She looks up at Robin.

Helena (*very softly*) *Did* Michael give it to her?

Pause. Robin does not reply. Helena sighs deeply, rises, and crosses to the window

Robin Don't go near the window, please?

Helena stops and turns towards Robin. From above we hear a muffled cry of surprise. Then, throughout the following, we hear scampering

Helena Did he?
Robin Linda says you're to be quiet.
Helena (*calmly*) She said you were to keep me quiet. What would you do if I started to scream? (*Pause*) You needn't worry. I shan't do that now. But I want to look out of the window. (*She moves towards the window*)

Robin No...

Robin raises the knife and steps towards Helena. Helena turns and looks at Robin. Pause. Helena then turns her back to him again and moves to the window. Robin watches helplessly as she looks out over the drive

Helena What time is it? (*She looks at Robin*)

Robin shrugs

Helena Nothing to tell the time by but your sister?

There is a pause during which we hear feet clattering down the stairs, past the door, and then down again

Robin Please stay away from the window.
Helena Why are you so afraid of her?
Robin Ssssh.
Helena Why shouldn't you talk to me? You're my son.
Robin I——
Helena "We are your children, anyway". You said that.

The main door downstairs slams shut

Robin Please keep away from the window.
Helena (*looking out through the window*) She's showing them to the main gate. Three of them. They're so young. They can't have twenty-one years between them. (*She turns and notices Robin's anxious look*) All right. (*She moves away from the window*) Better? Poor Robin. You *did* need me. What *will* you do when she leaves you? She *will* one day.
Robin She won't leave me. She *does* care. You — you might not think so, but I know it. She pretends she doesn't — but she does.
Helena You couldn't bear to be abandoned twice, could you? She wants you to think she cares. Don't you see? So that you'll kill me for *her. She* wouldn't do it. You will be the one if necessary, won't you?
Robin I'll tell you something. It — it was my idea. It was. All mine. I said I'd kill you for Linda. We're together.
Helena Linda said you cared for me. Don't you?
Robin Why should I? Have you ever cared for me?
Helena I've thought of caring for you.
Robin You hate me.
Helena Linda told you that.

Robin No. You said you had no children. I was there. *We* were there. Linda and me, standing in front of you and you said you had no children.

Helena Oh Robin, what else could I say? What alternative had I? You leave nothing to yourself. It's all Linda's viewpoint. Of course I loved my children. I wanted children badly. When I married Peter I knew that because of my abortion I would never be able to have any more. The only children that would ever be mine were you and Linda. I *had* to pretend that I hated children, so that I could forget what I had done to myself. And it worked. I convinced myself that I had never even had a child until today. Until you made me believe what did happen. Cruel. You're both very cruel. I — (*She almost breaks, but controls herself*) When I knew, and I saw you, standing there — twenty-one years of living without any help from me — how do you think I felt? A son, more than anything, and no claim at all. Trite things — ridiculous things like reading to you — first days at school — first days at work — bandaging knees — tucking you up in bed — buying you things. Somebody else had done them. Somebody who couldn't care as much as I would have cared. I had no claim — even your names. I've never thought of you as — Robin and — Linda. I — and — I — I was proud of you. I — I listened as you said all that you thought of me. I wanted you to stop — and yet go on, waiting for that one spark of knowing that I wasn't so bad. But everything I said to heal — to show that I wasn't all those things, was smashed. Every hope I'd ever had proved groundless. Everything about me and my life shown to be worth less than nothing.

Silence

Robin He might come.
Helena Perhaps.

Pause

Robin (*gently*) I hope he does. (*Pause*) Really.
Helena Because you don't want to kill me or because you don't want me to die? You'll be brave again with Linda. (*Pause*) I want you to promise me something, Robin.
Robin Yes?
Helena (*taking a silk square from her handbag*) If Michael doesn't come, and if I were brave enough, then I would kill myself. But I'm like you. I'm not very brave. (*She shows Robin the silk square*) If I'm

alone at ten o'clock, I want you to take this piece of silk and fold it like this... (*She folds it, to show him, then places it around her neck as though to strangle herself*) And I want you to know that you are doing it, not because of Linda, but because I *asked* you to. I won't struggle and I won't make a sound. Now — take it.

Robin takes it

And remember, for me — not for Linda.

The door downstairs slams shut. Then there is a silence in the room. Robin looks at Helena, who is now quite calm

Helena You promise?

Robin nods

Say it.

Robin I promise.

We hear Linda's footsteps on the stairway. Robin looks amazed at Helena

Helena I mean it.

A key is turned in the lock and the door opens. Linda appears. Robin suddenly moves across the room to Linda

Robin Leave the door open.
Linda What?
Robin Move away from the door. Leave it open.
Helena (*gently*) Robin...
Linda I see. (*To Helena*) What did you promise him? A home? A family? Or — what? (*To Robin*) Get out of my way.

Linda turns the key in the lock. Suddenly Robin lashes out and slaps her across the face again and again

Helena Robin!

The key drops to the floor and Robin picks it up. He unlocks the door and flings it open, pointing the knife at Linda

Robin (*to Helena*) Go on, get out — quickly!

Helena remains still

It's no trick. The door's open.
Linda She won't leave.
Robin Go on!

Helena moves across to Robin

Helena I've got to stay, Robin. She's right. Don't you understand? I
must know.

*Robin stares at Helena, stunned. Linda takes the key from Robin, quite
easily, and re-locks the door. Linda looks at Robin. She is shaken. She
rubs her hand over her face, where he hit her*

Linda Right. I was *right*!

*During the following tirade Linda crosses to the shutters and one by
one, she closes them all, except the one nearest to the ante-room door*

I should never have trusted. Never. Learn your lesson. Learn your
lesson. I never cared, that's what you said — that's what you believed.
Why? Why didn't I? Because I knew that — through all your talk
— through all you said — that you didn't really care enough for
me. Well now, *now* I don't care for anybody. Do you hear? I don't
give a sod for you, Robin. You can rot! *Rot*! (*To Helena*) And you
— you think that Michael loves you — is that what you're waiting
for? Why should *you* be sure. Why should *you* be sure of anything?
Why? I couldn't be sure of anybody — of anything — and I've made
sure that you'll never know — that your — that your certainty will
be *nothing*! (*She moves to Helena*) It's nearly ten o'clock. Nearly
time. It matters to you, oh, how it matters! What would life be like
not knowing, eh? I never *knew* Michael cared for me — I never
knew *you* cared for me — and Robin! Robin I thought I knew — but
Michael was the one — *Michael*!

There is a pause. Silence

Come here, Helena.

Helena goes to Linda. Thirty seconds silence

And Robin. Robin — come here.

Robin goes to Linda. Linda puts them both in a position facing the ante-room door.

Are you ready, Robin?

Thirty seconds silence

Helena He — he doesn't. He...
Linda Ten o'clock. (*She takes a key from her pocket, which she fits into the lock of the ante-room door*) He came this morning.

Linda turns the key and opens the door. For a split second we see the viciously mutilated body of a man standing upright, before it slumps into a heap across Helena's feet. Helena lets out one chilling scream of anguish as she recognizes Michael

Helena Michael!

There is then complete silence but for Helena's sobbing as she kneels on the floor, cradling Michael's head. Then Linda starts to laugh, softly. The laugh becomes tears and she weeps

Linda He loved her. He brought the necklace. He loved her...

Helena backs away from the body, suddenly sickened by it. She rises and backs to the wall. Linda calms herself, sobbing to a silence

You mother-bitch. Suffer. You — you mother-bitch!
Helena (*pleading*) Robin...

Linda unlocks the main door. She opens it

...please?

Linda closes the final shutter. The only light now is from the doorway. Robin is terrified. Linda moves into the door light

Linda Kill her, Robin. (*She offers Robin the knife*) Kill her or leave her. Kill the cause — or leave the mother-bitch with her stud.

Robin backs to the door

Helena Please — be brave for me, Robin...

Linda opens the door wider for Robin

Linda Then leave her.

Linda leaves the room, but is visible beyond the doorway. Robin is about to follow her when suddenly he grabs the knife from Linda and rushes back into the darkness. We see Robin's vague outline as he pauses in front of Helena

Robin The knife. I'm sorry.

Robin stabs and stabs, again and again. There is no sound at all from Helena. Robin rises and blunders to the doorway. He slings the knife into the room. He is sobbing. As he reaches the door he stops and looks at Linda, who is standing in the door light. Suddenly Linda slams the door shut and locks it from the outside. There is a silence, before we hear Linda's feet descending the stairway. The room is in total darkness. Robin lets out one long agonised cry of terror

Linda...!

THE END

FURNITURE AND PROPERTY LIST

On stage: Table. *on it:* **Handbag**. *in it:* a small, oblong jewellery-box containing a beautiful sapphire necklace, wrapped in gaily coloured paper. A knife. 2 small cards. A pen. A packet of cigarettes. Lighter. **Briefcase**. *in it:* Gift-wrap paper. Sellotape. Nail scissors. Ribbon-bow. Papers. Notebooks. A letter
Two chairs
Small circular rug
Old tea chest
Large, soft canvas travelling bag with an unzipped zip-top, with a garment protuding from it.

Personal: **Linda**: cigarette and lighter, Ante-room door key
Robin: loose change, a packet of cigarettes (*in coat pockets*)
Helena: wrist-watch

Offstage: Small gift-wrapped package containing a cheap necklace and a card (**Robin**)
Handbag. *in it*: Cigarettes in a case. Cigarette lighter. Silk square (**Helena**)

LIGHTING PLOT

Practical fitting required: nil
One interior setting

To open: Darkness

Cue 1	**Linda** opens the staircase door *Light comes in through the door*	(Page 1)
Cue 2	**Linda** closes the staircase door *Darkness*	(Page 1)
Cue 3	**Robin** opens the staircase door *Light comes in through the door*	(Page 2)
Cue 4	**Linda** opens the shutters *Early morning light comes in through each window as the shutters are opened*	(Page 3)
Cue 5	**Linda** closes all but one of the shutters *The lighting dims window by window*	(Page 48)
Cue 6	**Linda** opens the staircase door *Light comes in through the door*	(Page 49)
Cue 7	**Linda** closes the remaining shutter *Only the light from the door remains*	(Page 49)
Cue 8	**Linda** slams shut the staircase door *Darkness*	(Page 50)

EFFECTS PLOT

Cue 1 The staircase door closes (Page 1)
*Hollow footsteps climbing a stone staircase which stop
behind the door during the silence after* **Linda** *has
extinguished her cigarette*

Cue 2 **Linda**: "Just behave as we've planned." (Page 10)
The main door slams shut downstairs

Cue 3 **Linda** and **Robin** exit (Page 11)
*Steady sound of feet mounting a stone staircase.
The footsteps approach the door and come to a halt*

Cue 4 **Robin**: "No, I don't believe you——" (Page 42)
The main door slams shut downstairs

Cue 5 **Linda**: "Sssssh!" (Page 42)
*Footsteps scuffling on the stairs.
Banging on the door of the room underneath*

Cue 6 **Linda**: "Be quiet!" (*Pause*) (Page 43)
Footsteps approach the door

Cue 7 **Helena**: "Mich——!" (*Pause*) (Page 43)
The door knob is rattled backwards and forwards

Cue 8 **Robin** looks at **Linda** puzzled. **Helena** reacts (Page 43)
The sound of someone running upstairs

Cue 9 **Girl**: (*off*) "'S locked as well." (Page 43)
*The door is rattled again. Through the next passage
we hear footsteps coming up the stairs and
approaching the door*

Cue 10 **2nd Girl**: (*off*) "You sure?" (Page 43)
The door is rattled again

Cue 11 **Boy**: (*off*) "*Look out!*" (Page 43)
The sound of stampeding feet as the **Boy**
and the **Girl** *run upstairs*